Navigating Challenges

A Story of Overcoming Workplace Adversity

By: Regina Watts

Contents

Introduction 2

Chapter 1 Workplace Labels and Identity 9

Chapter 2 From Despair to Rejoicing: Overcoming Challenges 14

Chapter 3 The First Call: A New Opportunity 19

Chapter 4 The Second Call: A Turning Point 26

Chapter 5 Decisions, Decisions: Weighing the Options 32

Chapter 6 Probation Officer or Financial Technician: A Crossroad 37

Chapter 7 Decision Day: The Path Becomes Clear 44

Chapter 8 The Final Decision and A New Chapter .. 47

Chapter 9 Embracing the Role of Financial Technician 52

Chapter 10 The Unexpected Call: Becoming a Financial Analyst 58

Chapter 11 Navigating Employee Rights and Assistance Programs (EAP & RA) 64

Chapter 12 Document, Document: The Power of Recordkeeping 72

Chapter 13 Challenging Interactions and Behavioral Styles 78

Chapter 14 Coping with Difficult Situations: Tools and Strategies 85

Chapter 15 Conclusion: Growth Through Adversity and New Beginnings 95

Personal Reflection 100

Glossary 108

Templates 112

Workplace Documentation Template 112

Communication Strategy Worksheet 114

Goal-Setting Template 116

Introduction

In life, the path to success is rarely a straight line. It is often marked by unexpected challenges that test our resolve and shape our character. In "Navigating Challenges: A Story of Overcoming Workplace Adversity," I invite you to join me on a personal journey through the ups and downs of my professional life. This story chronicles the transformation from hardship to triumph, highlighting the pivotal moments that defined my career and strengthened my resilience.

Professional life can feel like navigating a complex maze filled with unexpected turns and hidden obstacles. Each twist and turn presents new challenges and opportunities for growth. Many of us enter the workforce with dreams, aspirations, and a clear vision of success. However, reality often diverges from those expectations. It is within this divergence that the essence of our journey is found.

I was filled with excitement and hope when I first entered the workforce. My dreams were vivid and expansive, painted with ambition and determination. I envisioned a career where I could make a difference, contribute meaningfully to my organization, and rise through the ranks, earning respect and admiration from colleagues. This dream was not just about personal success; it was about having an impact.

However, reality soon set in. While full of promise, the workplace also presented challenges I had not anticipated. I encountered a variety of personalities, each with their own agendas, and quickly realized that the corporate world was not solely based on merit. External factors, often beyond one's control, could influence success or failure. This realization shattered my initial perceptions and forced me to confront the complexities of organizational life.

Adversity in the workplace can take many forms, from interpersonal conflicts to systemic issues that affect employee morale. These challenges may arise from leadership disputes, team dynamics that hinder collaboration, or the struggle to maintain personal values in the face of pressure to conform. Understanding these challenges is the first step toward navigating them effectively.

Workplace conflict is often unavoidable. It arises from differing perspectives, competing priorities, and various levels of experience. For me, these conflicts were not just complex; they were enlightening. They forced me to reflect on my own values and beliefs, prompting me to ask critical questions about my place within the organization. Why did certain interactions leave me feeling drained? What could I learn from these experiences?

The complexities of workplace dynamics often leave individuals feeling isolated and unsure. I often grappled with feelings of inadequacy, uncertain about asserting myself in a competitive environment. Navigating these dynamics required me to understand interpersonal relationships and organizational culture better. It became essential to discern when to advocate for myself and when to step back and reassess.

Amid these challenges, a vital lesson emerged: the importance of resilience. Resilience is not just about bouncing back from setbacks; it's about growing and evolving through adversity. It requires a mindset shift—a willingness to embrace challenges as opportunities for growth rather than seeing them as insurmountable obstacles.

Resilience is often mischaracterized as an inherent trait that only a few possess. It is a skill that can be cultivated through experience, reflection, and intentional practice. It involves developing emotional intelligence, fostering a positive mindset, and building a support network of allies who can offer guidance and encouragement during difficult times.

Each challenge I faced became a catalyst for personal and professional growth. I began to see adversity not as a stumbling block but as a stepping stone toward greater self-awareness and empowerment. Each conflict taught me valuable lessons about my own strengths and weaknesses and underscored the importance of standing firm in my convictions.

A significant part of my journey involved learning the art of advocacy—for myself and others. In the face of adversity, I discovered the power of speaking up and challenging the status quo.

Initially, advocating for myself felt foreign and uncomfortable. I was conditioned to avoid confrontation and prioritize harmony over honesty. However, I realized that staying silent often perpetuated dissatisfaction. By learning to express my needs and set boundaries, I began to reclaim my voice and assert my presence in the workplace.

As I gained confidence in advocating for myself, I also recognized the importance of standing up for others. Advocacy is not just a personal endeavor; it is a collective one. Supporting others in their struggles fosters a sense of community and strengthens the workplace culture. I actively mentored others, encouraging them to find their voices and share their experiences.

One of the most profound lessons I learned was the power of vulnerability. In a world that often values strength and stoicism, embracing vulnerability can feel counterintuitive. However, I found that acknowledging my own struggles and emotions opened the door to deeper connections with others.

Being vulnerable requires courage—the courage to admit when things are difficult, to share fears and uncertainties, and to seek help when needed. In moments of vulnerability, I found support and a renewed sense of purpose. Sharing my experiences with others created a ripple effect, encouraging colleagues to do the same and fostering an environment of openness and understanding.

Through vulnerability, I forged authentic connections with colleagues. These relationships became invaluable sources of support during challenging times. When we share our struggles, we humanize ourselves and create an atmosphere where empathy and compassion can thrive. This shift transformed my workplace into a more supportive and inclusive environment.

As I navigated the storms of my professional life, I learned the importance of celebrating small victories. No matter how minor, each triumph became a building block for resilience and motivation.

In a world that often emphasizes prominent achievements, it's easy to overlook the significance of incremental progress. Each time I overcame a challenge—whether through a difficult conversation, implementing a new idea, or supporting a colleague—I consciously tried to recognize and celebrate that achievement. These moments served as reminders of my growth and capability.

Celebrating small victories helped me cultivate a positive mindset. Rather than dwelling on setbacks or failures, I began to focus on my progress. This shift in perspective allowed me to approach challenges with renewed energy and optimism. I realized that resilience is fueled not just by overcoming adversity but also by appreciating the journey itself.

In sharing my experiences, I hope to illuminate the lessons learned in the face of adversity. This narrative is not just about the struggles I faced; it is a celebration of the large and small victories that emerged from those challenges. Through resilience and determination, I learned that every challenge holds the potential for transformation, and it is often in our darkest moments that we find the light to guide us forward.

As I reflect on my journey, I see a tapestry woven from threads of hardship, triumph, and personal growth. Each challenge contributed to my evolving identity, shaping me into who I am today. I stand as a testament to the power of resilience and the belief that we can navigate the storm and emerge stronger than before.

Join me as I recount my journey, a testament to the power of resilience in the pursuit of a fulfilling career. I hope that by sharing this story, I can inspire others facing their challenges to embrace their journeys, find strength in vulnerability, and transform adversity into opportunity. Together, let us navigate the storm and celebrate the victories along the way.

Chapter 1

Workplace Labels and Identity

When I first entered the professional world, I quickly realized that what people called me mattered—a lot. These weren't just names or titles; they were markers of who I was in that space. To others, I wasn't just "me"—I was the sum of my actions, my reputation, and those labels that got whispered in meetings or listed on email chains. Sometimes, I was "the go-to person," and other times, "the cautious one." And each label, good or bad, carved out a specific place for me in the workplace.

In my early days, the labels seemed pretty straightforward. You're given a title, and that's how you introduce yourself. "Hi, I'm [Name], a Junior Analyst." But it didn't take long for me to understand that the title on my business card was just the beginning. What truly mattered were the informal reputations we all carried around, like invisible name tags that everyone could see except ourselves.

Being called "reliable" was like wearing a golden badge—doors opened, opportunities flowed, and trust followed me into each new project I was given. That label stuck, and it felt good. It meant I was the one chosen to lead a critical initiative, the one who could handle a challenge when the stakes were high. But then there were other labels, ones that weren't as flattering. I once overheard someone describe me as "too cautious," and even though they hadn't meant it harshly, it was a blow. It shaped what came next, as people started to pass me over for opportunities that demanded quick, bold decisions.

I began to realize that these labels were like tools—they could either build up my career or fence me in, depending on how I handled them. For a while, I wore "rising star" like armor, and it made me feel unstoppable. That label opened up a network of mentors and opportunities that might have remained hidden otherwise. Yet, the same system that had lifted me up could also hold me back when my perceptions changed.

I didn't want to be boxed in, so I decided to take control. First, I started by understanding what these labels meant—where they came from and how people saw me. This meant a lot of conversations. It wasn't easy to ask colleagues, "How do you perceive me?" or "What do you think are my strengths and weaknesses?" But that discomfort was the first step. It showed me how I could take those perceptions and either amplify them or actively work to change them.

If a label began to limit me, I took action. When people thought of me as "too cautious," I started volunteering for projects that needed a different side of me—something that showed initiative and a willingness to take risks. I wasn't about to let that single perception define my future. I worked hard to rebrand myself, not with empty words but through action, showing those around me that there was more to me than the cautious choices of the past.

There was also power in speaking up for myself. Sometimes, you have to remind others of your achievements. Not in a boastful way but in a way that lets them know that the effort, the dedication, and the results are there. I learned to advocate for myself, to make sure that my contributions were recognized because if I didn't, no one else would.

Yet, despite all of that—the self-awareness, the rebranding, the advocating—there were times when I didn't get what I thought I deserved. I worked for it, put in the hours, exceeded expectations, and felt that the promotion was within my grasp. But it slipped away, given to someone else who maybe hadn't worked as hard. I remember the sting, the feeling of being overlooked. It's easy to let bitterness take root in moments like that.

But I found solace in a different perspective, one that wasn't rooted in the office, or in titles, or even in recognition. It came from something deeper, something that reminded me that my efforts weren't just for human eyes. In those moments of disappointment, I remembered what Paul wrote in 1 Corinthians: "I have planted, Apollos watered; but God gave the increase." It reminded me that my work, my growth, wasn't entirely in my hands. Yes, I could work hard, I could plant and water, but ultimately, it was about trusting that recognition and reward would come in their own time, in a way I might not expect.

In 2009, when I transitioned from the military to a civilian government job, I thought my path was clear. I had served as a Sergeant, moved up the ranks with dedication, and earned my degrees. I thought the trajectory was simple: work hard, get rewarded. But life isn't that straightforward. Despite my qualifications and my readiness, the opportunities I craved didn't always come when I wanted them. It was humbling, and at times, I questioned if all the work was in vain.

Looking back, I see that it wasn't a wasted effort. Every struggle, every label, every missed opportunity has been a lesson. They taught me resilience. They taught me that my value wasn't confined to what others saw in me at that moment. The labels others assign to us are powerful—they can lift us up or hold us down—but they're not set in stone. I could shape them, change them, and, most importantly, I could decide how much power they held over my story.

So, here's my reflection: the labels we carry and the roles we play are all part of a larger journey. Each perception others have of us is just a moment in time, not the whole story. And while I work to reshape my labels, I remember that true growth, the kind that matters most, is something beyond what others can give me—it's a gift, a reminder that my efforts are seen, even if the reward doesn't come when or how I expect it.

Chapter 2

From Despair to Rejoicing: Overcoming Challenges

In 2009, I found myself standing at a metaphorical edge, staring into an abyss where all I could see was uncertainty and defeat. Life had crumbled beneath me in ways I hadn't imagined, leaving me feeling lost and overwhelmed. It was as if everything I had carefully built was suddenly slipping away—my plans, my dreams, the very ground that had once felt so secure. I was left with nothing but fear, facing what seemed to be a bottomless fall into despair. But it was from this dark place that my journey began, a journey that would teach me resilience, faith, and the power to find light even when the world seemed to go dark.

I want you to walk with me through those days—not to relive the heartbreak, but to understand the hope that eventually followed. My story isn't just about the struggles; it's about how I stumbled, how I fell, and, ultimately, how I rose again.

My descent into despair truly began that year. I had left the military in 2003 to pursue an education. It was a choice driven by hope—a decision to create a better future for myself and my family. But as I soon found out, the journey was anything but easy. Balancing my studies while being a parent was already a challenge, but life had more trials in store for me. As I neared graduation, the ground seemed to collapse completely: I lost my job, faced eviction, and, on top of it all, I was expecting another child. In every direction I turned, another door closed. It felt like all the weight I was carrying—the responsibility of providing for my family, of finishing school, of just surviving—was crushing me, piece by piece.

I remember one night in particular, the anxiety swelling so much that I felt like I couldn't breathe. I had reached my limit, and in that breaking moment, all I could do was cry out for help. I called out to God, not knowing if anyone or anything would answer. It wasn't a miraculous shift, not something you see in movies where everything just magically becomes okay. But slowly, in small ways, there was a change. It was as if a tiny spark had ignited inside of me—a warmth that, while faint, brought a sense of hope where there had been none. It wasn't a dramatic rescue. Instead, it was a quiet, steady light that slowly began to grow.

During those dark days, I turned to scripture for strength. I found solace in Romans 15:13, which spoke of hope and peace through faith. "Now the God of hope fill you with all joy and peace in believing, that ye may abound in hope." The verse was like a lifeline. It reminded me that my situation, no matter how dire, wasn't the end of my story. It spoke of a hope that went beyond what I could see or understand at that moment, and it reminded me that faith was not about the immediate outcome—it was about trusting in a bigger plan, even when all seemed lost.

It wasn't easy, but I started to rebuild. Piece by piece, I worked on putting my life back together. I graduated that year and, despite everything that had happened, began training to become a probation officer. It felt like a small victory in the midst of all the chaos. It was proof that no matter how deep the fall, there was always a way to climb back up, even if it was just one step at a time.

Looking back, the real triumph wasn't that I graduated or got a job. The real victory was the shift that happened inside me. The transformation wasn't just in my circumstances—it was in my perspective. I learned that my strength wasn't just in my achievements but in my ability to keep moving forward, even when everything felt impossible. I began to see each obstacle as a challenge that could make me stronger, not as something meant to break me. The joy I eventually found didn't come from external success. It came from knowing that I had endured the worst and was still standing.

That journey from despair to rejoicing is something deeply personal, but I think it's also something we all share in some form. We all face moments where we feel like everything is falling apart. And it's in those moments that we discover who we truly are. It's when we fall that we find out just how strong we can be when we get back up. I learned that resilience isn't about never feeling afraid or hopeless—it's about feeling those things and continuing on anyway.

So, as I share this part of my story, I hope it resonates with you. I hope it reminds you that even when you're at the edge of that metaphorical cliff, staring into what seems like an endless abyss, there's always a way forward. There's always a light, no matter how faint, that can lead you out. Our challenges shape us, and it's in overcoming them that we find true growth and true joy.

Each setback isn't the end—it's a setup for something greater, a chance to learn, to change, and to emerge stronger than before.

Chapter 3

The First Call: A New Opportunity

The clock on the wall ticked louder than usual, echoing through the sparsely furnished apartment that I called both my home and makeshift office. Outside, the sky was overcast, a blanket of clouds casting a persistent shadow that mirrored my growing despair.

There I was, surrounded by stacks of job applications, each rejection adding weight to the silence that filled the room. Once steaming and hopeful, my coffee had settled into a tepid reminder of the morning's unsuccessful job hunt.

But then the phone rang.

I stared at it for a moment, the shrill ring slicing through the quiet. My heart quickened, a mix of hope and hesitation gripping me. I reached out, hands trembling slightly, and picked up the receiver.

"Hello?" "Ms. Watts, this is Karen from the Department of Probation and Parole." The voice was crisp and professional—a tone I had become all too familiar with over the past few weeks. "I'm calling regarding the position you interviewed for last week."

My pulse quickened. I held my breath, bracing myself for another polite decline. But instead, she continued.

"We're pleased to inform you that we would like to offer you the probation officer position."

My mind spun as her words sunk in. I clutched the phone tighter, my knuckles turning white. "Are...are you serious?" I managed to stammer, not fully believing my ears.

"Yes, Ms. Watts, I'm serious. We've reviewed your qualifications and were impressed with your background and interview performance. Congratulations."

A flood of relief and gratitude washed over me. I had imagined this moment so many times, but now that it was happening, I struggled to find the right words. "Thank you," I finally said, my voice quivering. "You don't know what this means to me."

Karen's voice softened. "We're looking forward to having you on board. I'll email you the official offer and details. Please respond within 48 hours."

"Thank you again," I repeated. "I...I won't let you down."

As I hung up, I felt a surge of emotion I hadn't experienced in months. Hope—a feeling I thought I had lost—began to seep back into my life. I sank into my chair, clutching the phone like a lifeline. This was it—my second chance. The opportunity to build a career that I had fought so hard for was finally within my grasp.

But the initial wave of euphoria was quickly followed by a flood of anxiety. Memories of past disappointments flashed through my mind like lightning. I had seen opportunities slip through my fingers before and faced the hollow emptiness of rejection. Could I truly trust this moment? Would it lead to the stability I so desperately needed, or was it just another illusion?

For years, I moved from job to job, position to position, hoping each time that I finally found my place. From my early days as a police dispatcher to my stint as a corrections officer, I had constantly strived to prove myself. Each role had its challenges—each came with its own set of storms that left me questioning my worth, my path, and my choices. Yet, I persevered, pushing forward with a determination that was both a blessing and a curse. I had hoped that my sacrifices, my long hours, and my relentless pursuit of excellence would one day pay off.

This call felt like the answer to years of prayers. Still, I couldn't ignore the doubts that crept in. What if this opportunity slipped away like the others? What if, once again, the promise of stability dissolved before my eyes? I could feel the familiar weight of fear beginning to settle in, tugging at the edges of my newfound hope.

I stood up and walked to the window, staring out at the rain, tapping softly against the glass. It reminded me of the many nights I had sat here, watching the city lights flicker, wondering when my break would come. This small apartment had witnessed countless nights of frustration, tears, and desperate prayers whispered into the darkness. It had become a sanctuary—a place where I could release my worries, yet it was also a reminder of the battles I faced daily.

As I gazed at the rain-soaked street below, I whispered a quiet prayer of thanks. I didn't know where this path would lead, but I knew I had to trust the process. I had to believe that this opportunity was different. After everything I had endured, I owed it to myself to embrace this moment of victory, no matter how uncertain the future seemed.

I found myself replaying the call in my mind over and over. The words, "we would like to offer you the position," echoed in my head like a melody, each repetition soothing the doubt that threatened to rise. I thought back to my time in the military—the sense of purpose and structure it had given me. The feeling of camaraderie, the knowledge that I was part of something bigger than myself. After leaving that world, I had searched endlessly for a similar sense of belonging, and I wondered if this new role could finally fill that void.

Slowly, I walked back to my desk and picked up my journal. Flipping through the pages filled with goals, prayers, and reflections, I found a blank space. I wrote the date at the top and began to pour out my thoughts. The words flowed easily, a mix of gratitude and determination. I wrote about the long nights, the moments of doubt, and the strength it took to keep moving forward. And then, as the ink flowed, I wrote the most important line of all: This is my time. I will not let fear hold me back.

After closing the journal, I felt a sense of calm settle over me. I knew that challenges lay ahead—there always would be. The road to success was never a straight line but rather a winding path filled with obstacles that could either break you or build you. And as I looked around my small apartment, I felt a quiet sense of pride. This space, though modest, had become a symbol of my resilience. It had been my refuge, my battleground, and now it was the place where I would start anew.

I picked up my phone again, this time to call my mom. As her familiar voice filled the line, I felt the weight of years lift just a little. "Mom," I said, a smile tugging at my lips, "I got the job."

The words felt surreal, but saying them aloud made it real. Her excitement on the other end of the call was contagious, and for a moment, the clouds outside seemed to part. As we spoke, I could feel a renewed sense of strength and purpose building within me. This was more than just a job offer; it was a lifeline, a reminder that even when the storm rages, there is always hope on the horizon.

And so, as the call ended and the rain continued to fall, I knew that this was just the beginning. There would be more storms and challenges, but I was ready this time. I would navigate whatever lay ahead with faith as my anchor and determination as my guide.

The path wasn't clear, but it was mine, and I was ready to walk it.

Chapter 4

The Second Call: A Turning Point

The air in my apartment still hummed with the excitement of the first call, like a small but steady flame burning against the backdrop of my uncertainty. I had told my mom, and she was thrilled—a wave of relief had washed over both of us. For the first time in months, I felt a lightness that was both unfamiliar and exhilarating. I was finally beginning to see the pieces of my life falling into place.

But life can test your resolve just when you think you've found your footing. And, as if on cue, the phone rang again.

I glanced at the clock—it had only been a few hours since the first call. My pulse quickened, and a slight chill crept over me. Part of me feared it was Karen calling back to say there had been a mistake and that the offer wasn't real. Taking a deep breath, I steadied myself and reached for the phone.

"Hello, this is Regina Watts."

"Good afternoon, Ms. Watts. This is Cynthia from the finance department at Veterans Affairs. You interviewed for the Financial Technician position a few months ago, and we wanted to follow up."

I paused, caught off guard. The Financial Technician position? The one I had applied for months before? The details of that interview had long faded into the blur of applications and rejections. I steadied my voice. "Yes, I remember."

"Well, Ms. Watts, we are pleased to offer you the position. It's a term position, initially for 12 months, with the possibility of becoming permanent based on performance. The starting salary is $37,000, and we believe your background and skills would be an excellent fit."

My head spun. Two job offers in one day. I felt a rush of emotions—gratitude, confusion, and an overwhelming sense of responsibility. This position offered more stability in the short term compared to the probation officer role, but there was no guarantee of permanence. Yet, the modest salary was still a lifeline, and the possibility of staying beyond the year was tempting.

I hesitated, realizing that I was standing at a crossroads. "Thank you, Cynthia," I said, choosing my words carefully. "I'm grateful for the offer. Can you give me a little time to think it over?"

"Of course," she replied. "We understand it's a significant decision. Please let us know within 48 hours."

A heavy silence settled over the room as I hung up the phone. Two paths lay before me—both promising yet uncertain. I had spent so much time praying for a single opportunity; now I had two. But the choice wasn't as simple as it seemed.

I sank into the chair by the window, staring at the rain as it continued its rhythmic dance against the glass. The Financial Technician position came with stability—a steady paycheck and the chance to gain experience in finance, an area that could open up a range of career opportunities. But it was temporary, and the probation officer role, though it felt like a calling, didn't offer the same security. What if I chose wrong? What if the wrong decision set me back years, dragging me into another cycle of struggle?

The questions swirled in my mind, each one louder than the last. I needed clarity, and I needed it quickly.

I closed my eyes, recalling the prayers I had whispered in the darkest of nights, asking for guidance, for a sign that things would get better. This wasn't how I had expected those prayers to be answered—with a choice between two futures that both felt uncertain. But as I sat there, something else became clear: this was an opportunity to trust myself and make a decision that wasn't just about survival but about stepping into a future I believed in.

I reached for my Bible, the familiar pages worn from years of use. I flipped to Proverbs 3:5- 6, a passage that had always anchored me: "Trust in the Lord with all thine heart; and lean not unto thine own understanding. In all thy ways acknowledge him, and he shall direct thy paths."

I knew what the passage meant—I had read it countless times—but living it, truly trusting that I would be guided in the right direction, was a different story. I needed to lean into faith, to trust that even if the path was uncertain, it was leading somewhere meaningful. I needed to believe that every experience, twist, and turn was shaping me for something greater.

I took a deep breath and decided to make a list—a habit I had developed in the military when I needed clarity.

I grabbed a notebook and split the page in two, writing "Probation Officer" on one side and "Financial Technician" on the other.

Under each heading, I listed the pros and cons, carefully weighing the benefits and potential risks.

Probation Officer:

- *Pros: A chance to follow my passion for criminal justice, stability in the long term, and an opportunity to make a difference in people's lives.*
- *Cons: Lower starting salary, physically and emotionally demanding, potential risk if the position didn't work out.*

Financial Technician:

- *Pros: Immediate financial stability, valuable experience in a new field, and potential stepping stone to a permanent role.*
- *Cons: Term position with no guarantee of permanence, a shift away from my passion, and uncertainty about future opportunities.*

I stared at the page, feeling no closer to an answer. Each option had its own set of challenges and rewards. It was then that I realized the decision wasn't just about logic. It was about faith—faith in myself and faith that the path I chose, even if uncertain, would ultimately lead me where I needed to be.

The second call had been more than just another job offer; it was a turning point. It was a reminder that sometimes the most important decisions are the ones that force us to step into uncertainty, trusting that, despite the storms, we will find our way.

Chapter 5

Decisions, Decisions: Weighing the Options

The sky outside cleared, and the rain gave way to the golden hues of a late afternoon sun. It cast a warm glow across the apartment, illuminating the scattered papers, notebooks, and coffee cups that had become my companions in these long, uncertain weeks. The soft light created a sense of calm, a brief respite from the storm of thoughts swirling in my mind.

Sitting at the small table by the window, I stared at the two offers in front of me. Both were written on crisp white paper, official and intimidating. I had hoped the sunlight would make the decision feel clearer, but all it did was highlight the weight of the choice ahead of me.

Each offer represented a different path—one that felt like a leap of faith and another that seemed like the practical choice. The probation officer role offered purpose and passion, a chance to fulfill my desire to make a real impact in the criminal justice field. It was the kind of work I had always envisioned myself doing. But it also meant stepping into the unknown, with a lower starting salary and an uncertain path ahead. It would be emotionally demanding and physically exhausting.

On the other hand, the Financial Technician position at Veterans Affairs promised immediate stability. The salary would ease some of the financial strain that had brewed over the past months, and it offered the kind of security I hadn't felt in years. But it was also a temporary solution, a term position with no guarantees. While finance wasn't my passion, it was a field I could navigate—one that could provide new skills and opportunities if I chose to pursue it long-term.

I leaned back in my chair, running a hand through my hair as I sighed. My head felt heavy, as if weighed down by the potential consequences of each choice. It was easy to feel trapped, caught between my desire for passion and purpose and my need for security and stability.

I thought about my family—about my mom, who had always believed in me, and my children, who depended on me for a better future. The stakes were high, and every decision felt like it carried the weight of all my past struggles and sacrifices. This was more than just a job; it was about reclaiming a sense of purpose and control over my life.

I reached for my journal, the one that had been a constant companion throughout my journey. Flipping to a blank page, I began writing. I wrote about the doubts, the fears, and the hopes that accompanied each option. Putting the words on paper made them real, and in some ways, it lightened the burden, allowing me to see the situation from a distance.

As I wrote, I realized that this wasn't just about making the "right" choice. It was about defining my values and aligning my decisions with them. I had spent so many years reacting to circumstances, trying to stay afloat, that I had lost sight of my long-term vision. This decision was an opportunity to reclaim that vision, to choose a path not just based on necessity but on where I truly wanted to go.

After a few minutes, I set the pen down and took a deep breath. The sunlight continued to pour in, bright and hopeful. I closed my eyes and allowed myself a moment of quiet, tuning out the noise of my thoughts. In that silence, I found myself praying, asking for clarity and strength. I needed to believe that whatever path I chose, I would find a way forward, that I would rise to the challenge and make the most of it.

As I sat there, I remembered a conversation I once had with a mentor during my time in the military. "The toughest choices are the ones that reveal who we are," he had said. "They test your values, your courage, and your faith." His words echoed in my mind, and I knew that this moment was one of those defining choices. It wasn't just about a job; it was about choosing the kind of life I wanted to lead.

I opened my eyes, and the sunlight seemed to shine a little brighter. I knew which path aligned with my heart and my purpose. The Veterans Affairs position, though initially daunting, offered me the chance to serve others in a meaningful way. It was an opportunity to make a difference in the lives of those who had served our country and step into a career that resonated with my values.

I stood up, feeling a resolve settle within me. By choosing to work with Veterans Affairs, I could enjoy a rewarding career with excellent benefits, opportunities for growth, and the satisfaction of knowing that I was contributing to something greater. The financial security offered by the position was a significant draw, but beyond that, the fulfillment of a purpose-driven career made this choice the right one. This was not just about stability—it was about building a life that mattered, knowing I was making a difference every day.

Later that evening, I reached for my phone as the sky turned to a deep, dusky blue. My fingers hovered over Karen's number for a moment before I dialed. When she picked up, I felt the nerves tighten in my chest.

The road ahead would not be easy, but it would be mine. And with each step, I was ready to prove to myself that I could navigate the storm, no matter how fierce it became.

Chapter 6

Probation Officer or Financial Technician: A Crossroad

The day slipped into evening, and the sun's golden hues faded into a deepening twilight, casting long shadows across the apartment. The stillness around me felt heavier now as if the weight of the decision hanging over me intensified with each passing hour. The choice between becoming a probation officer or a financial technician was more than a professional dilemma—it was a test of everything I had come to believe about myself and the life I wanted to build.

I stood in the center of the room, looking down at the two printed job offers spread out on the table like maps of two different futures. The stark black text on the crisp white pages felt almost ominous as if the decisions they represented carried the power to change everything. I knew I couldn't put this off any longer. It was time to confront the reality of the choice before me. I pulled up a chair and sat down, resting my hands on the edge of the table. I took a deep breath, focusing on each role individually, stripping away all the external noise and considering what each path truly meant.

I started with the probation officer position, which had ignited a spark of excitement when Karen first called. This opportunity aligned with my long-held passion for criminal justice, the career I had envisioned when I decided to leave the military and pursue an education. I knew that being a probation officer meant more than just a job; it meant becoming an advocate, a guide, and sometimes, a last chance for people who had veered off course. It meant making an impact in a tangible, meaningful way.

But with that impact came responsibility. The demands of the role were clear—late nights, high emotional stakes, and the reality of working with individuals who had faced some of life's darkest moments. I had read stories of probation officers who became burnt out, worn down by the relentless cycle of criminal behavior and the emotional toll it took. Was I prepared for that? Could I handle the intensity of the work without it overwhelming me?

I thought about my time in the military and the resilience I had built there. The structure, the discipline, and the sense of purpose had given me strength, and I had thrived in that environment. But this role, while fulfilling, wasn't about enforcing rules or following orders. It required empathy, patience, and the ability to see beyond someone's mistakes to the potential for change. It required me to be a source of strength for others.

I felt a mix of excitement and fear as I considered this future. I knew it would challenge me in ways I hadn't been tested before, but it also held the promise of becoming the career I had always dreamed of—a calling that would push me to grow, to lead, and to make a difference.

Next, I turned my focus to the Financial Technician offer. There was no denying the appeal of the immediate stability it offered. A guaranteed paycheck, structured hours, and the chance to work in a controlled and predictable environment. The idea of financial security was alluring in a life that had seen so much uncertainty. With two children to support and bills piling up, the practical choice seemed obvious.

The finance field was not unfamiliar to me. It was a skillset I developed over time, navigating budgets and managing finances at home and in my previous roles. While it wasn't a passion, it was something I could excel at—a stepping stone that could potentially open doors to other, more lucrative opportunities. The prospect of gaining stability, even if only for a year, was a safety net I couldn't ignore.

Yet, every time I considered taking this path, a sense of discomfort crept in. It felt like choosing comfort over passion, practicality over purpose. The more I thought about it, the more I realized that this role, while secure, would take me further from the career I truly wanted. I had spent years trying to build a life around my passion for criminal justice. I had sacrificed, studied, and worked for this dream. Was I willing to let it go now for a short-term sense of security?

The clock on the wall ticked steadily, marking the time as it slipped away. I felt the pressure of the deadline—48 hours to decide. But beyond the deadline was the deeper realization that this choice was about more than just these two jobs. It was a crossroads that demanded I be honest with myself about who I was and what I valued. I stood up, walked to the window, and gazed out at the city. The lights sparkled against the darkness, each representing someone else's story or journey. For years, I had been so focused on surviving, on doing what was necessary to stay afloat. But this moment felt different. It was an opportunity to choose a path based not on fear but on faith and a sense of purpose.

In that quiet moment, I remembered a lesson I had learned early on in my career: sometimes, the safest choice isn't the best choice. Growth happens when you take risks, step out of your comfort zone, and trust that your passion will sustain you, even when the road gets tough. The financial technician position was not just an easy choice—it was the right choice for me at that moment. It offered the stability and security I needed, but more importantly, I believed that God had a plan for me, even though my true passion lay in criminal justice. I had come to realize that following that passion, while fulfilling in some ways, might have negatively impacted my mental well-being in the long run.

As I reflected on my decision, I felt a sense of peace. This role as a financial technician provided an opportunity to grow and serve in a meaningful capacity, and it aligned with the current needs of my life. It wasn't about settling—it was about trusting the path ahead and knowing that I could still make a difference in this role while also preserving my mental health and overall well-being.

The following morning, I woke early. The sky was clear, and the sun bathed the apartment in a warm glow that felt like a sign—a promise that I was moving in the right direction. I picked up my phone and dialed Cynthia's number. My fingers felt steady, my mind clear.

"Cynthia, this is Regina Watts," I said. "*I wanted to let you know that I am officially accepting the financial technician position.*"

Her response was immediate and enthusiastic. "We are so glad to have you, Regina. I'll send over the next steps and training information."

After hanging up, I took a deep breath and exhaled slowly. The decision was made, and for the first time in a long while, I felt a sense of clarity and purpose. I knew the road ahead would not be easy, but I was ready to face it with everything I had.

As the day went on, I felt a weight lift from my shoulders. Choosing the Financial Technician role was a commitment to my passion and my calling. It was a choice to trust myself, to believe that no matter what challenges came my way, I had the strength and resilience to navigate them.

I folded the probation officer's offer carefully and set it aside. It was a reminder that sometimes, the hardest decisions are the ones that define us. I had chosen the path that aligned with my spirit. By choosing to become a financial technician, I knew I was stepping into a role that offered both stability and purpose. And as I prepared for the journey ahead, I felt ready—knowing that I could weather anything with faith and purpose guiding me.

Chapter 7

Decision Day: The Path Becomes Clear

The day had arrived. After weighing the options, seeking guidance through prayer, and reflecting on my journey, I made the decision that felt right for my future. The position of Financial Technician was not just another job; it was an opportunity, a doorway to stability and growth for me and my family. Accepting the offer was a moment of clarity that allowed me to take control of my path and trust in the journey ahead.

As I sat in my apartment, the anticipation of what lay ahead filled me with both excitement and a sense of peace. I knew this decision was not just about accepting a role; it was about embracing a new chapter where I could thrive, build, and grow. I took a moment to look back at the storms I had faced—disappointments, financial struggles, and moments of deep uncertainty. Each one had been a stepping stone, preparing me for this very moment.

Choosing this role felt different. It wasn't about settling but rather seizing an opportunity to grow in an environment that appreciated my skills and hard work. I realized that God's plan for my life might not always align with my expectations, but it is often in these unexpected moments that we find our true path. The scripture from Proverbs resonated deeply with me: "Trust in the Lord with all your heart, and lean not on your own understanding" (Proverbs 3:5-6). I had done my part—acquired the education, honed my skills, and remained resilient in the face of challenges. It was time to trust that the doors opening before me were meant for my growth.

When I received the call offering me the position, I accepted it with a sense of gratitude. The woman on the other end of the line congratulated me, and I thanked her warmly, knowing that this was the next step I needed to take. As I hung up the phone, I felt a wave of motivation. This was a new beginning—one where I could apply my skills, build a solid foundation for my future, and, most importantly, create a stable environment for my children.

With the decision made, I prepared for the journey ahead. I looked forward to immersing myself in the role, eager to learn and grow. I reflected on the words from the attachment: "It is not the storm that defines us, but how we choose to navigate it." This sentiment echoed in my mind. Accepting the position was my way of navigating the storm—of turning uncertainty into a pathway for growth and transformation.

The opportunity to be a Financial Technician was more than a job; it was a chance to demonstrate resilience, apply the skills I had honed in previous roles, and contribute meaningfully to the organization. I was determined to walk this path with purpose, using every experience to build my future.

As I looked out the window, I felt a sense of peace. The morning sun shone brightly, and I whispered a prayer of gratitude. I knew that while the road ahead would have its own set of challenges, I was ready. This role was not just about stability; it was an opportunity to redefine my path, gain new skills, and create a brighter future for myself and my family.

With each step forward, I reminded myself that it's not just about where we end up but how we choose to walk the journey. The decision was made, and with it came the motivation to embrace this new chapter with confidence, faith, and a steadfast belief that the best was yet to come.

Chapter 8

The Final Decision and A New Chapter

"The future belongs to those who believe in the beauty of their dreams."

~Eleanor Roosevelt

The morning sunlight poured into the room, casting a golden glow that felt like a promise of new beginnings. For the first time in months, I woke up feeling the weight of uncertainty lifting from my shoulders. The decision was made, and a renewed sense of purpose and determination came with it. I had chosen the path that aligned with my heart and passion: I was going to become a Finance Technician.

The journey to this point was not an easy one. It was marked by countless moments of doubt, disappointment, and tears. Each setback and rejection felt like another weight pulling me down, challenging my faith in myself and my dreams. But I refused to let the obstacles define me. I learned through my experiences that resilience isn't about avoiding the storm; it's about finding the courage to stand tall and face it head-on.

I took a moment to breathe deeply, reminding myself of a lesson I once read: **"God gives the increase."**

I had done the work—years of education, training, and preparation. Now, it was time to trust that my efforts would be rewarded, not by chance, but through faith and perseverance. The journey tested my patience and my resolve, but it also showed me that my growth was not in vain.

I reached for my journal, flipping to the entry where I had poured out my hopes and fears. I wrote again, this time with clarity:

"I am walking into this new chapter with faith, knowing that no storm is too strong when I am guided by purpose."

The act of writing solidified my commitment. It felt as if I was reaffirming a pact with myself—to stand firm, to trust in God, and to believe that He would lead me down the path that was best for me. I trusted that every step, even the painful ones, had brought me to this moment for a purpose.

As I sat at the small table by the window, I reflected on the path that had led me here. The military, the schooling, the struggles as a single parent—all those experiences had shaped me into a person capable of resilience. They were not failures; they were stepping stones that prepared me for the responsibility I was about to take on.

The truth is the crossroads between becoming a probation officer and a financial technician was not just about choosing a job. It was about choosing a life. It was about embracing a vision of myself as someone who could make a difference, not just earn a paycheck. It was a decision to walk in alignment with my values And pursue a career where I could serve those who have sacrificed their lives to protect us all. As a financial technician, I would be contributing to the well-being of veterans, ensuring they receive the support they deserve, rather than managing those who have committed a crime as a probation officer.

I thought back to a passage from the Bible that had carried me through many hard times: "Trust in the Lord with all your heart and lean not on your own understanding." (Proverbs 3:5-6).

It reminded me that while I couldn't see the entire path ahead, I could trust that each step was leading me where I needed to be. Even in the uncertainty, there was a purpose; even in the waiting, there was preparation.

The sunlight continued to stream through the window, and as it did, I whispered a prayer of gratitude. This was more than just the beginning of a new job; it was the start of a new chapter where I could build, grow, and become the person I was destined to be. I reminded myself that the road wouldn't always be smooth. There would be difficult days, moments when doubt would try to creep back in. But I was prepared. I had been through storms before, and each time, I had come out stronger.

I stood up, looking around the apartment that had been both my sanctuary and my battlefield. It was here that I faced my doubts, made my plans, and ultimately, chose to rise above the fear. I knew that every storm had its purpose, and this one had transformed me. The sunlight felt warm on my face, a reminder that there is always light, even in the darkest moments.

As I packed my bag for the first training session, I thought about the lessons I had learned—about perseverance, faith, and trusting the process. I had faced rejection, uncertainty, and fear, but I had also found strength, resilience, and hope. I was no longer the person I had been at the start of this journey. I was stronger, more determined, and ready to face whatever challenges lay ahead.

This was the beginning of a new chapter—a chapter where I would walk in faith, serve with passion, and grow into the person I was meant to be. With every step forward, I was reminded that the beauty of the journey is not in how easy the path is but in how we choose to navigate it. I had navigated my storm, and now, I was ready to walk boldly into the light.

Chapter 9

Embracing the Role of Financial Technician

"The road to success and fulfillment often winds through unexpected paths."

My journey to becoming a Financial Technician was anything but straightforward; it was filled with growth and transformation. Initially, I faced this role with uncertainty, but over time, I recognized it as a vital step in both my professional and personal life.

Letting go of my earlier ambition to become a probation officer was challenging. I had dedicated years to studying criminal justice, completing corrections officer training, and interning at probation offices. This career path had become a part of my identity, and the thought of shifting directions was daunting. However, when the opportunity to become a Financial Technician arose, I viewed it as a chance to explore a new path that could still offer purpose and growth.

I recalled a vital lesson from my career: sometimes, a detour is actually leading us to where we need to be. The financial role, while different from my original goal, was filled with potential. It demanded diligence, problem-solving abilities, and a knack for navigating complex systems—skills I had developed in the military and through my education.

Reflecting on my past challenges, I realized they had prepared me for this moment. Disputes with leadership and navigating tough workplace dynamics had not just been obstacles; they were valuable learning experiences that built my resilience. This new role allowed me to apply my existing skills while developing new ones, like financial analysis and technical expertise, which would further enhance my professional toolkit.

My work was not just about numbers; it was about understanding the stories behind those numbers and supporting veterans in managing their benefits accurately. I began to see my role as a meaningful contribution, even if it differed from my initial vision. The emphasis on resilience and adaptability reminded me that I could find fulfillment in unexpected ways. As I embraced this new mindset, I discovered that growth often comes from the most surprising places. While the role required attention to detail and precision, it also allowed me to engage with my analytical side—transforming complexity into clarity. The skills I honed in previous roles—leadership, communication, and a strong work ethic—were transferable and valuable across various fields.

Over time, I found my rhythm in the Financial Technician role. My initial doubts faded as I recognized that this was not about abandoning my dreams; it was about equipping myself to pursue them when the time was right. I continued to take on challenging projects and attended training sessions to expand my knowledge. This chapter of my career was not what I had planned, but it was precisely where I needed to be.

I learned that success is not merely about reaching a predetermined goal; it's often about finding value and purpose in the journey. Each experience, whether it aligned with my original plans or not, became a building block in my career. I was grateful for the opportunity to grow in ways I hadn't expected. My initial position quickly transitioned into a permanent role. Trusting in God's guidance helped me navigate obstacles and turmoil. For three years, I flourished in this role, becoming the go-to person whom leadership relied on for important tasks. I earned the trust of my superiors and was given assignments typically reserved for team leads and supervisors. My leadership valued my input, and I became a respected employee who strived for success.

However, when my lead accepted a new position, a storm began brewing within the team. This upheaval disrupted the harmony we had built. Our director left, and a new one, Paul, took over. His arrival brought a shift in dynamics, and I sensed that the strong foundation I had established might be at risk.

Despite the challenges posed by Paul, I remained confident in the relationships I had built. My past experiences had equipped me with resilience, and I was determined not to let this new energy undermine my progress. Though Paul's leadership style was troubling, I continued to perform my duties with integrity and transparency.

As I navigated this tumultuous period, I noticed comparisons being made between me and a new employee. While I stood firm in my commitment to doing what was right, this colleague appeared more focused on pleasing Paul. Our differing work ethics became evident during team meetings, but I was undeterred, knowing I had the knowledge and experience to excel.

After a rigorous interview process, I was confident that I had secured the promotion to lead the team. However, the unexpected happened: the new employee was awarded the position instead. I was devastated, and so were my supervisor and coworkers, who were shocked by the decision. Despite my disappointment, I approached the new employee and congratulated her.

In the following days, a supervisor from another team expressed his understanding of my qualifications and performance, explaining that my honesty had led to a lack of trust in Paul. This revelation was disheartening, but I chose to accept the situation rather than pursue an EEO complaint.

Without the support of my supervisor, I felt isolated as coworkers distanced themselves from me, fearing they might become targets, too. However, I maintained a positive attitude, believing that the storm would eventually pass. I knew that God was watching over me, and I was determined to navigate this challenge with grace.

Despite the adversity, I greeted everyone with a smile each morning. Unfortunately, Paul seemed to take issue with my positivity, wanting to see me broken instead. Yet, my faith remained steadfast. I found strength in biblical promises, believing that I would overcome this situation.

As Paul's hostility grew, I was reassigned to a small office, which exacerbated my claustrophobia and made it impossible for me to perform my duties. Recognizing the toll this was taking on my well-being, I reached out to the director of the organization for assistance. Eventually, I was offered a new position, though it came with a pay cut.

With tears in my eyes, I accepted the change, realizing it was necessary for my mental health. I left my previous role without goodbyes, feeling like a scapegoat. Yet, just a week later, I received an offer for a new job that would double my salary and guarantee annual raises.

Chapter 10

The Unexpected Call: Becoming a Financial Analyst

"The road less traveled often leads to the most profound growth."

When I decided to embark on a new journey, it meant leaving the comfort of my home and the familiar faces of my family. I traveled over 600 miles to embrace new opportunities, hoping for a fresh start and a path that would lead me closer to my dreams. Initially, everything seemed to fall into place. I secured an accounts receivable position and later moved into a finance technician role. I even explored positions in criminal justice and military settings, trying to find my true calling. For a while, I believed I had found my path.

But life has a way of surprising you when you least expect it. After only a month in a lower-paying role, I received a call that changed everything. It was a shock, an unexpected turn that pushed me out of the position I thought was my stepping stone. In that moment of uncertainty, I felt a wave of disappointment. Had all my efforts been for nothing?

Reflecting on my journey, I realized that my path was far from a straight line. It was winding, filled with twists and turns that challenged my resolve. But amidst this uncertainty, I understood that it was my path, uniquely designed for me. The detours and setbacks were not signs of failure; they were moments that tested my faith and built my resilience. I chose to embrace this understanding, recognizing that the journey to success is rarely predictable.

When the opportunity to become a Financial Analyst presented itself, I was filled with a sense of excitement and anticipation. It felt like the culmination of all my previous experiences—each role, each challenge, had prepared me for this new chapter. The transition was smoother than I expected, largely because a former colleague was on the team. Having someone familiar with whom to collaborate provided comfort, and it made stepping into the role easier. My new coworkers were eager to share their experiences, both the highs and the lows of working for the company. While there were some unfavorable aspects, I made a conscious decision to focus on the positive.

My main objective was to grow, both personally and professionally. I believed that by concentrating on the good and staying proactive, I could make meaningful strides in my career. I immersed myself in understanding the team's operations from Monday to Friday and throughout the year. I committed to learning every aspect of what made the company successful. I wanted to grasp the entire journey, from the initial stages to the final outcomes, to contribute effectively and make a meaningful impact.

As I dove deeper into my responsibilities, I found myself motivated to learn and improve. I remained dedicated to my work, always striving to provide exceptional service to both internal and external customers. I eagerly took on projects and engaged in training opportunities, knowing that these experiences would enhance my skills and prepare me for future promotions. Forward-thinking had become a fundamental part of my approach. I understood that being proactive was essential—not just in my professional life but in my personal and spiritual journey as well.

By staying ahead and anticipating potential challenges, I felt more in control of my path. I knew that being prepared allowed me to navigate through life with greater ease, seizing opportunities as they arose. It was an empowering mindset that kept me moving forward.

However, after a few years of smooth sailing, the storm clouds began to gather. The company struggled with keeping supervisors on the team, and leadership refused to promote anyone from within the team. This caused tension, leading to resentment and gossip. I could hear the murmurs of discontent, but I chose to remain focused. My strategy was to keep a positive attitude and stay busy. I enrolled in classes, sought hands-on experience, and told myself that if I stayed engaged, the storm would pass over me.

But as time went on, the brewing storm turned into a full-blown tornado. Approved training programs were suddenly disapproved, projects were dismantled, and the gossip grew louder. The path I had fought so hard to build was being threatened, and it became clear that the storm wasn't going anywhere. It had settled in, and I needed to brace myself for the impact.

One day, I found myself in the crosshairs of Director Michelle. She targeted my career, and as she did, my coworkers distanced themselves from me. The people I thought were my friends revealed their true colors, joining in on the whispers and the gossip. I felt isolated, realizing that the support I thought I had was an illusion. But this time, I was stronger. I had weathered storms before, and I knew how to stand my ground.

It wasn't easy, but I resolved to fight back. With a smile on my face and a calm demeanor, I let Michelle know that I would no longer tolerate the abuse. I began documenting everything, sending letters to her boss, and escalating my complaints. When these efforts led to no resolution, I sought help from the union. Although I won some battles, I soon realized that the union, like the company, had its limitations. Nepotism and alliances ran deep, and I needed to seek outside help.

Determined not to let this tornado uproot my career, I hired an attorney. I knew that I had the right to defend my position, and I stood on truth, believing that justice would prevail. No one would push me out of the position I had worked so hard to attain. I had navigated storms before, and I was ready to navigate this one with the same resilience, faith, and strength that had brought me this far.

The path was far from easy, but I knew that every step, every decision, was leading me closer to where I was meant to be. I was committed to walking this journey, knowing that success wasn't always straightforward, but it was uniquely mine.

Chapter 11

Navigating Employee Rights and Assistance Programs (EAP & RA)

Understanding employee rights is crucial for every worker, whether a supervisor or a team member. Navigating the complexities of workplace policies and assistance programs can be daunting, but having a clear understanding of your rights and available resources can make a significant difference in how you manage conflicts and challenges in your career.

Employee Rights

It's essential to familiarize yourself with your rights as an employee, beginning with the policies set by the company you work for. While some companies provide employee handbooks outlining these rights, not all do, as they are not legally required. Therefore, when considering employment, it's important to take into account whether or not a company offers such a handbook.

If an employee handbook is available, it is vital to read it thoroughly. The handbook often includes critical information such as legal compliance measures, the company's code of conduct, and methods for conflict resolution. Knowing this information equips you with the tools needed to navigate disputes, misunderstandings, or conflicts that may arise in the workplace. Familiarizing yourself with these details allows you to use this resource effectively when necessary. If your company does not offer a handbook, you will need to rely on company policies as your guide.

Handbooks serve as a foundation for employees, providing clarity on company expectations and employee rights. They also act as a safeguard, offering legal guidance that can help protect both the employer and employee. This proactive approach ensures that all parties are informed and prepared to handle conflicts in a way that promotes understanding and resolution.

Accessing Employee Support Programs

Beyond handbooks and policies, various organizations—including state and federal agencies as well as corporate entities—offer a range of resources designed to support employees. Programs such as

Employee Assistance Programs (EAP), reasonable accommodations (RA), exchange programs, mediation services, hardship transfers, and alternative dispute resolution (ADR) are essential tools for maintaining a productive and supportive work environment. Understanding these resources and how to access them can play a critical role in safeguarding your rights and ensuring a balanced and supportive workplace.

If you ever find yourself in need of these services, don't hesitate to reach out to your supervisor or human resources officer. Utilizing these programs can be vital in protecting your employment and well-being.

Employee Assistance Program (EAP)

The Employee Assistance Program (EAP) offers consultation, short-term counseling, and other resources to help employees manage personal or professional concerns that may impact their productivity and well-being. These services are often available at no cost to eligible federal employees and their immediate family members. In addition to supporting employees directly, EAP services also provide consultations for supervisors, aiding them in their efforts to assist employees more effectively.

Having access to EAP services can be transformative, as they offer confidential and supportive counseling to address various challenges, such as stress, mental health concerns, and work-life balance issues. The program is designed to provide tools and strategies that help employees regain focus and well-being, which in turn enhances their performance and overall job satisfaction.

Reasonable Accommodation (RA)

Reasonable accommodation refers to adjustments or modifications in the workplace that allow individuals with disabilities to perform their job duties effectively. These accommodations ensure equal employment opportunities by creating a supportive environment tailored to meet the needs of each employee.

Examples of reasonable accommodations include flexible work schedules, ergonomic adjustments, assistive technology, and modifications to job responsibilities that enable employees with disabilities to contribute fully to the workplace. Understanding and requesting reasonable accommodations can be essential in creating an inclusive and supportive work environment that values each individual's contributions.

Exchange Programs

Exchange programs are structured initiatives that enable employees to temporarily or permanently take on different roles, either within their department or in different organizations. These programs allow employees to gain new skills, experiences, and perspectives.

By participating in an exchange program, employees have the opportunity to broaden their skill set, foster collaboration across departments, and enhance their overall professional development. These programs can also facilitate knowledge sharing, promote teamwork, and increase an organization's adaptability by encouraging a more versatile and informed workforce.

Mediation Services

Mediation services are conflict resolution programs designed to help employees and employers address workplace disputes through the involvement of a neutral third-party mediator. The goal of mediation is to facilitate open communication, foster understanding, and reach a mutually acceptable resolution without resorting to formal disciplinary actions or legal proceedings.

Mediation can be a valuable resource for resolving conflicts in a constructive and non-confrontational manner. It allows both parties to express their concerns openly and work toward a solution that respects everyone involved. Utilizing mediation services can prevent minor disputes from escalating into larger, more complex issues, preserving relationships and maintaining a positive work environment.

Hardship Transfers

A hardship transfer program provides employees with the flexibility to relocate or transfer to a different position or location within the organization due to personal or family hardships. This support aims to assist employees facing significant challenges such as medical issues, family emergencies, or other circumstances that impact their ability to perform their duties in their current role or location.

Hardship transfers demonstrate an organization's commitment to employee well-being by offering a compassionate approach to addressing personal challenges. Understanding this program's availability and eligibility criteria can help employees and supervisors make informed decisions when such situations arise.

Alternative Dispute Resolution (ADR)

Alternative Dispute Resolution (ADR) programs offer structured processes for resolving workplace conflicts without resorting to traditional litigation or formal grievance procedures. ADR includes various methods, such as mediation, arbitration, and negotiation, all aimed at achieving a mutually acceptable resolution in a more efficient and cost-effective manner.

ADR can be an effective tool in minimizing workplace disruptions and fostering a culture of open communication and collaboration. By engaging in ADR, employees and employers work together to resolve issues through dialogue and mutual understanding, avoiding the stress and expense associated with more formal conflict resolution methods.

Understanding your rights and the available support programs as an employee is essential for creating a balanced and supportive work environment. Whether through the use of employee handbooks, EAP services, reasonable accommodations, or mediation programs, knowledge is a powerful tool that can transform challenges into opportunities for growth. Taking the time to familiarize yourself with these resources not only empowers you to navigate difficult situations but also ensures you are prepared to take control of your career and well-being.

Chapter 12

Document, Document: The Power of Recordkeeping

Throughout my career, I learned that documentation is not just a bureaucratic necessity; it is a powerful tool for protecting one's rights and integrity. When I faced challenges in the workplace, particularly when taking legal action against my employer, my meticulous habit of keeping records became my greatest asset. I knew that to win my case, I needed to be prepared with evidence—every claim backed up, every conversation documented.

From the moment I filed my lawsuit, I documented everything. Every email, every conversation, and every statement from leadership was recorded and organized. I knew that, much like a card game at a family cookout, this was a battle of strategy. I was determined to have every card in my favor, so I meticulously kept every piece of evidence that could back my claims.

Initially, when I informed the leadership of the lawsuit, they dismissed my statement, brushing it off as a bluff or scare tactic. They believed it would blow over and that I wouldn't follow through. But two years after my initial complaint, the truth surfaced. All parties involved were summoned to provide depositions, and one by one, they had to give statements on record. It was a turning point in the case, and their initial confidence began to waver.

As they testified, I watched them lie, claiming not to know who I was or insisting that they never caused me harm. Their arrogance suggested that they thought the case would disappear. But I was $20,000 deep in legal fees and emotionally drained from the battle. Despite this, I was ready to drain my account to fight for justice. Armed with my documentation and proof, I remained steadfast.

> **"In the face of adversity, documentation becomes your strongest ally."**

By the time the depositions took place, I was six years into the company and three years into the complaint. It's hard to describe what it feels like to perform your duties successfully while simultaneously battling leadership. It requires immense mental strength to withstand each hit without breaking. I often felt like David going up against

Goliath, standing firm in faith and armed only with the truth.

The story of David from 1 Samuel 17:50-53 has always inspired me. Just as David faced the giant with nothing but a sling and a stone, I, too, faced my giant with documentation and faith. Despite the odds, I believed in my fight for justice, knowing that with determination and resilience, I could overcome the obstacles in front of me.

My persistence led me to seek sanctions against the company. The record of the investigation was so deficient that it failed to present an impartial and appropriate account of events. An appropriate factual record is essential, as it provides a basis for determining whether discrimination occurred. However, the investigator did not even contact relevant individuals who could have provided insight into the more favorable treatment others received. Management officials were not questioned regarding these standards or their differential treatment.

At the core of my complaint was the company's continuous failure to accommodate my disability. Management claimed that they engaged in an interactive process, but the report of investigation (ROI) failed to identify who performed the assessment, what was discussed, or the outcome. The company asserted that an assessment of my essential functions was conducted, yet no results were disclosed.

To address this, I moved to sanction the agency for not providing an appropriate, impartial factual record, arguing that this deficiency would prejudice my pursuit of the complaint. This failure forced me into additional expenses related to discovery, including interrogatories, document requests, and depositions. I also sought sanctions in the form of attorney fees to cover these discovery costs.

The day finally arrived when we all appeared before the judge. One by one, members of management entered the courtroom, suited up and ready with their rehearsed stories. It was clear they had coordinated their testimonies, presenting a unified front. But despite their collective strategy, I remained hopeful. I knew the truth was on my side.

As the trial proceeded, I held back tears, staying strong until one leader testified that, given all the evidence, he would not have handled the situation differently. When asked if he would have made a different decision, his response was a firm "No." At that moment, I could no longer hold back the tears. The emotional toll of fighting for justice, only to hear the same dismissive attitude, was overwhelming. I stepped out of the courtroom to compose myself before returning.

When I reentered the room, an informal decision had been made. The judge, attorneys, and I discussed a potential settlement. It was then that I knew—I had won my case. The relief was palpable; I had fought hard, and my persistence had paid off.

That same day marked the last for my director, who was allowed to retire immediately. Others involved in the case also either retired or moved to different positions shortly after. The settlement included a compensable amount, attorney fees, and a new work arrangement that granted me 100% telework. With the departure of those who had wronged me, the company's new leadership was unconnected to the lawsuit, offering a chance for peace in my work environment.

After the lawsuit, I chose to stay with the company for another four years. Despite my reservations about promotions, knowing I had a lawsuit against the company, the new leadership reassured me that my past would not hinder my future. I decided to focus on enhancing my skills and growing within the company.

During those years, I completed the Leadership Program and the Inspiring Supervisor Program. I also took on a leadership role within my team, collaborated with other teams, and applied for two leadership positions on my team. However, each time, newer team members were awarded the roles. After the second rejection, I realized it was time to seek opportunities beyond my current position.

The power of recordkeeping was not just in winning my case but in maintaining my integrity and ensuring that the truth prevailed. Documentation became my shield, and my determination became my weapon. Through every challenge, I learned that preparation, persistence, and faith are critical when standing against injustice. In the end, I emerged stronger, ready for the next chapter of my journey.

Chapter 13

Challenging Interactions and Behavioral Styles

Dealing with challenging interactions is a fundamental skill in both personal and professional environments. These interactions often stem from misunderstandings, differing perspectives, or heightened emotions, making them difficult to manage. However, with the right strategies, you can navigate these situations with grace and turn potential conflicts into opportunities for growth and collaboration.

Understanding the dynamics of communication plays a crucial role in resolving tensions. Body language, tone, and context all significantly impact how a message is received. By recognizing these non-verbal cues and approaching situations with empathy and active listening, you can de-escalate conflicts and create an environment where open dialogue is possible. Maintaining a calm demeanor and showing a willingness to find common ground are key steps toward fostering healthier relationships and achieving productive outcomes.

This chapter explores various techniques for managing difficult conversations and interactions while delving into different behavioral styles. Recognizing and understanding these styles can help enhance communication, teamwork, and conflict resolution, allowing you to handle challenging interactions more effectively.

Behavioral Styles

Behavioral styles refer to the different ways people express themselves, interact with others, and approach tasks or challenges. These styles influence how individuals communicate and how they respond to conflicts. Understanding these styles can improve your ability to navigate difficult interactions and work effectively with others. The four primary behavioral styles are:

1. **Assertive**
2. **Aggressive**
3. **Passive**
4. **Passive-Aggressive**

Assertive Behavioral Style

The assertive behavioral style is characterized by the ability to express one's thoughts, feelings, and needs openly and honestly while respecting the perspectives and rights of others. This approach strikes a balance between being passive and aggressive. Assertive behavior fosters healthier relationships, improves communication, and boosts self-esteem.

Key Features:

- Able to calmly express needs
- Aware of boundaries and can set limits
- Direct without an edge
- Respectful of self and others
- Self-confident but not overbearing
- Willing to collaborate and cooperate

Aggressive Behavioral Style

An aggressive behavioral style involves expressing one's thoughts, feelings, or needs in a way that violates the rights of others. This behavior is often hostile or confrontational, leading to strained relationships and toxic environments. Recognizing and adjusting aggressive behavior can pave the way for healthier communication and better interpersonal dynamics.

Key Features:

- Accuses others
- Blames and criticizes others for problems or conflicts
- Uses direct confrontation with loud or intimidating tones
- Disrespect others' feelings, opinions, and rights
- Interrupts conversations
- Intimidates others with sarcasm or controlling tactics

Dealing with Aggressive Behavior:

- Slow down the pace of communication
- Listen actively without reacting
- Leave the room if you feel threatened
- Speak in a neutral tone
- Avoid arguing or apologizing unnecessarily

Passive Behavioral Style

A passive behavioral style is characterized by a reluctance or inability to express one's thoughts, feelings, and needs openly. People with this style often prioritize the desires of others over their own, resulting in a lack of assertiveness and long-term dissatisfaction. By learning more assertive communication strategies, individuals can empower themselves to express their needs and build healthier relationships.

Key Features:

- Avoids conflict, even when they disagree
- Overly dependent on others for validation
- Exhibits low self-esteem, doubting their worth
- Resentment builds due to unexpressed feelings
- Avoids eye contact and uses closed body language
- Allows others to make decisions for them

Dealing with Passive Behavior:

- Allow for silence and encourage open dialogue
- Use open-ended questions to invite engagement
- Brainstorm ideas together without judgment
- Don't assume passivity means a lack of opinion or ideas

Passive-Aggressive Behavioral Style

A passive-aggressive behavioral style is a form of indirect resistance to the demands or expectations of others. This behavior is often characterized by a façade of compliance while harboring underlying resentment or hostility. People with passive-aggressive tendencies struggle to express their feelings openly, leading to confusion and frustration in relationships.

Key Features:

- Appears cooperative but internally disagrees or resents the situation
- Avoids responsibility and often blames others for their behavior
- Focuses on problems without offering solutions
- Communicates indirectly through sarcasm or subtle digs
- Procrastinates as a way of resisting tasks
- Portrays themselves as a victim to elicit sympathy

Dealing with Passive-Aggressive Behavior:

- Avoid getting drawn into their stance
- Try to uncover the underlying problem and negotiate
- Shift to a problem-solving approach
- Set specific goals and hold the person accountable

Understanding these behavioral styles and learning how to navigate challenging interactions is crucial for fostering better communication and collaboration in any environment. Whether dealing with assertive, aggressive, passive, or passive-aggressive behaviors, the key is to approach each situation with empathy, patience, and an openness to finding solutions. Developing these skills not only enhances relationships but also strengthens your ability to handle difficult conversations in both your personal and professional life.

Chapter 14

Coping with Difficult Situations: Tools and Strategies

"It's not the load that breaks you down, it's the way you carry it."

~Lou Holtz

Difficult situations are inevitable, both in life and in the workplace. Whether it's managing a tough conversation, handling a conflict with a colleague, or dealing with a high-stakes project, how we cope with these challenges can shape not only the outcome but also our growth as individuals. The ability to navigate difficult interactions is not about avoiding conflict—it's about facing it head-on with the right tools and mindset.

Coping effectively with these moments requires self-awareness, empathy, and strategic thinking. By adopting the right approach, we can transform what feels like a roadblock into an opportunity for improvement and growth. In this chapter, we'll explore practical strategies for handling tough situations and discuss how to maintain composure and focus, even when the pressure is high. Whether it's in personal or professional contexts, these tools will empower you to handle the challenges that come your way with confidence and resilience. In this chapter, we will discuss practical strategies for assessing difficult situations, understanding our own reactions, and using assertive communication to address conflicts effectively. We'll also explore how to manage challenging interactions while maintaining composure and focusing on solutions rather than problems.

1. Assessing the Situation

When faced with a difficult situation, the first step is to assess what's happening. Take a moment to gather as much information as possible about the dynamics at play.

Questions to Consider:

- **Is the other person responding assertively, passively, or aggressively?**
- **Is this behavior part of a pattern?** Do you notice the person consistently reacting this way, or is this an isolated incident?

Understanding the behavior of others will give you valuable insight into their motivations and how best to respond. For example, if the person is being aggressive, it's important to avoid escalating the situation by responding in kind. If they're passive, you may need to encourage more open communication. Recognizing the behavioral style helps you choose the right approach for managing the interaction.

Common Behavioral Patterns:

- **Assertive**: This person communicates clearly and respects the boundaries of others while expressing their own needs.

- **Aggressive**: They may use harsh or confrontational language, disregarding others' feelings or rights.

- **Passive**: They avoid confrontation and may not express their thoughts or feelings, which can lead to internal frustration.

- **Passive-Aggressive**: They may outwardly appear cooperative while harboring resentment, often leading to indirect conflict or subtle digs.

2. Assessing Your Reaction

Once you've evaluated the other person's behavior, it's essential to turn inward and reflect on your own reactions. Often, our initial responses to difficult situations are influenced by emotions such as anger, frustration, or defensiveness. Taking the time to evaluate how you're reacting can prevent knee-jerk responses and help you approach the situation more calmly and constructively.

Questions to Consider:

- **What reaction am I having to this behavior?**

- **Is my reaction part of a familiar pattern?** Do you often react this way in similar situations?

- **Am I overreacting?** It's important to gauge whether your response matches the gravity of the situation.

- **What resources do I have to respond assertively?** Reflect on the tools you can use to stay calm and respond in a balanced way.

This self-assessment allows you to choose a more thoughtful and assertive response rather than reacting out of emotion. By recognizing patterns in your reactions, you can better control your emotional response and avoid escalating the situation.

3. Accepting the Situation

Acceptance doesn't mean resignation—it means acknowledging the reality of the situation and focusing on what you can control. Wishing the situation was different or obsessing over how things should have unfolded only adds to the frustration. Instead, focus on accepting the moment as it is, which allows you to think more clearly and take constructive steps forward.

Steps for Acceptance:

- **Stop wishing the situation were different**: Acknowledge what is happening and focus on how to address it.

- **Get emotional or physical distance**: If needed, step back from the situation temporarily. Take a short break, breathe deeply, or physically leave the room if safety or emotional overwhelm is an issue.

- **Slow down your breathing**: Calming your body helps to clear your mind. Inhale deeply and exhale slowly to reduce tension.

- **Take a timeout**: If emotions are running high, a short break from the situation can give you both time to cool down and reassess your approach.

Acceptance allows you to deal with the situation as it stands without letting emotions cloud your judgment. It also opens the door to a more measured and thoughtful response.

4. Strategizing an Approach

Once you've assessed the situation and accepted it for what it is, it's time to plan your response. This is where assertiveness comes into play. Assertive communication allows you to express your thoughts and feelings openly and respectfully without being aggressive or passive. It's about maintaining your boundaries while also being considerate of the other person's perspective.

Questions to Ask:

- **How can I use assertive behavior in this situation?**

- **Can I discuss the other person's behavior directly?** If so, what is the best time and place for this conversation? Timing and setting are key—having a difficult conversation at the right moment can lead to more productive outcomes.

- **If I cannot address the behavior directly, what other options do I have?** Are there other ways to manage or influence the situation without confronting it head-on?

In either case, remember to prioritize your well-being as you communicate. Assertiveness doesn't mean pushing through at all costs; it means choosing the right time, place, and method to address the issue while maintaining respect for yourself and the other person involved.

5. Addressing the Situation

When you're ready to address the situation, preparation is crucial. Walking into the conversation with a clear understanding of your goals and maintaining a respectful tone can help defuse tensions and facilitate understanding.

Steps for Addressing a Difficult Situation:

- **Step 1**

Prepare Your Thoughts: Before starting the conversation, take some time to organize your thoughts. Identify the main points you want to address so that the conversation remains focused and productive.

- **Step 2**

Use "I" Statements: This technique helps to express your feelings without placing blame. For example, instead of saying, "You always ignore me," try, "I feel undervalued when my contributions aren't acknowledged." This shifts the conversation from accusation to expression of your experience.

- **Step 3**

Be Clear and Direct: State the issue at hand clearly without sugarcoating it. Avoid vague language and address the problem directly, ensuring that the other person understands your concerns.

- **Step 4**

Maintain Your Composure: Emotions can run high during difficult conversations, but maintaining composure is essential for productive dialogue. Breathe deeply and pause if needed to keep the conversation focused and calm.

- **Step 5**

Listen Actively: Allow the other person to share their perspective without interruption. Validating their feelings—even if you don't agree—shows that you respect their point of view and can help to diffuse defensiveness.

- **Step 6**

Keep the Conversation Respectful: Even if disagreements arise, maintain a tone of respect throughout the conversation. Avoid personal attacks or negative language, and focus on finding a resolution rather than assigning blame.

Coping with difficult situations requires a blend of self-awareness, assertive communication, and a calm, strategic approach. By assessing both the behavior of others and your own reactions, accepting the reality of the situation, and planning an assertive response, you can handle challenges with confidence and composure. These strategies are not only essential for resolving conflicts but also for personal growth, as they help you navigate tough moments with resilience and maturity. Whether in the workplace or in your personal life, these tools will empower you to face difficult interactions head-on and emerge stronger on the other side.

Chapter 15

Conclusion: Growth Through Adversity and New Beginnings

As I reflect on my journey through the storms of my career, I have come to realize that resilience is not just about surviving the challenges—it's about embracing them as opportunities for growth and transformation. The trials I faced were not simple obstacles but rather stepping stones that led me to discover new strengths, refine my skills, and understand the depth of my own determination. Each setback, dispute, and difficult interaction became part of the intricate tapestry of my professional life, teaching me that the path to success is often uncertain and full of unexpected turns. Yet, it is in navigating those twists and turns that we find out who we truly are.

The moments of conflict with leadership, the isolation I felt during key battles, and the pressure of defending my rights in the workplace forced me to dig deep. I had to find the strength to continue even when everything seemed stacked against me. The pain, frustration, and moments of doubt were overwhelming at times, but they also became the fuel for my personal and professional growth. These challenges allowed me to develop skills I never knew I had—skills in diplomacy, communication, perseverance, and, most importantly, the ability to advocate for myself and others. Each challenge fortified my understanding of the importance of standing firm in my beliefs, knowing that there are times when we must fight for what is right, even when it feels like the odds are not in our favor.

One of the greatest lessons I learned was the significance of advocating not just for myself but for the rights of employees everywhere. There is immense power in knowing your rights, using your voice, and ensuring that others around you are treated with fairness and respect. Whether it was documenting every detail during a long legal battle or standing up to unfair leadership practices, I learned that advocating for justice requires both patience and persistence. It is not enough to know the law; one must have the courage to use it, navigate through complex workplace dynamics, and approach each conflict with grace, determination, and an unwavering sense of purpose.

Through the difficult experiences, I gained a deep understanding of workplace dynamics and how important it is to manage them with empathy and self-awareness. The storms I faced—while challenging—gave me invaluable lessons in leadership, empathy, and resilience. I came to understand that in any environment, but especially the workplace, communication is the key to defusing conflict and building meaningful relationships. Every interaction—no matter how difficult—offers the opportunity to connect, to learn, and to grow.

Today, I stand not only as someone who has overcome adversity but as someone who has thrived because of it. I have come to rejoice in the strength that I discovered within myself during the toughest times. I no longer see the challenges I faced as burdens but as catalysts for the growth I desperately needed. The adversity I endured helped me understand that success is not measured by the absence of hardship but by how we rise to meet those hardships head-on. I have learned that it is entirely possible to transform adversity into a powerful force for change, to rise above every challenge, and to inspire others to do the same.

Resilience, I have learned, is not simply an inherent trait—it is a choice we make every day. It is a conscious decision to keep moving forward when life gets hard, to face life's storms with courage, and to believe that, with faith and perseverance, we can weather any challenge. I have chosen resilience, and that choice has shaped every step of my journey.

As I bring this chapter of my story to a close, I carry with me a deep hope for others who are navigating their own storms. I hope they find the strength within themselves to persevere, to hold on to the belief that every challenge is an opportunity to grow, to learn, and to emerge stronger on the other side. Each storm, no matter how daunting, is temporary. What remains permanent is the resilience we build and the lessons we learn along the way.

I hope that my story encourages others to embrace their challenges with open hearts and determined minds, knowing that resilience will always guide us through. The road to success may not be smooth, but it is in overcoming obstacles that we find our greatest sense of achievement. My journey is far from over, but I look forward to the next chapter with hope, knowing that each step, no matter how challenging, is leading me toward a new beginning.

To those reading this, I offer a message of solidarity: continue to explore the challenges of your career with courage, compassion, and unwavering determination. Stand firm in your truth, trust in your abilities, and remember that growth often comes through the most difficult of trials. May your resilience shine through, and may you always emerge stronger, wiser, and ready for the next phase of your journey.

Personal Reflection

Chapter 1 Workplace Labels and Identity

The labels assigned to us at work can either lift us up or weigh us down. Over time, I learned that while we may not have control over what others think, we do have control over how we let those labels affect us. This chapter was a journey of realizing that my worth isn't defined by how others perceive me. I have the power to rewrite the narrative, embrace my true identity, and let my actions speak for who I am.

Chapter 2: From Despair to Rejoicing

This chapter made me realize that adversity is inevitable, but how we respond to it shapes who we become. Through moments of despair, I found strength in faith, learning to see every challenge as a stepping stone toward resilience. It's in these moments that we discover how capable we truly are. For me, these hard times were transformative, and I grew more determined to turn my struggles into something meaningful.

Chapter 3: The First Call

The first job offer brought both excitement and uncertainty. This chapter reminds me of the emotional rollercoaster that comes with change. I learned that even when we're unsure of what's ahead, taking that first step is crucial. Faith and trust in the journey were my anchors, and this moment became a symbol of hope—a reminder that every call, every opportunity, is part of a larger plan that may not be clear right away.

Chapter 4: The Second Call: A Turning Point

The second call was more than a job offer—it was a turning point in my personal and professional life. I realized that pivotal moments often come unexpectedly, and how we handle them defines the path we take next. I learned to trust my instincts, listen to my heart, and understand that sometimes, the hardest decisions lead to the greatest growth.

Chapter 5: Decisions, Decisions: Weighing the Options

This chapter was all about tough choices. I learned that no matter how difficult a decision may seem, clarity often comes from staying true to our values. The process of weighing my options helped me understand that success isn't just about financial security—it's about fulfillment and alignment with my deeper purpose. This reflection taught me that making the right choice sometimes means listening to my inner voice, even when it leads down an uncertain path.

Chapter 6: Probation Officer or Financial Technician: A Crossroad

Being at a crossroads was overwhelming, but it was also an opportunity for growth. I realized that while passion is important, so is mental and emotional well-being. Choosing the role that aligned with both my skills and my well-being reminded me that our career paths don't have to be rigid—they can evolve with us. This chapter helped me embrace the idea that sometimes, the "safer" choice can still lead to great personal satisfaction.

Chapter 7: The Final Decision and A New Chapter

Making the final decision felt like closing one chapter and opening another. In this chapter, I learned that embracing new beginnings requires both courage and faith. I let go of what I thought my path would look like and embraced where I was truly meant to be. This reflection reminds me that sometimes the journey surprises us, but it's those surprises that often lead to the greatest personal and professional fulfillment.

Chapter 8: Embracing the Role of Financial Technician

Once I embraced my role as a financial technician, I learned the importance of fully committing to the path I had chosen. This chapter was about accepting the responsibilities and opportunities that came my way realizing that growth happens when we dive fully into our roles. Embracing this role allowed me to serve others in meaningful ways, and I found fulfillment in being part of something larger than myself.

Chapter 9: Decision Day: The Path Becomes Clear

The clarity that came after making the decision to accept the financial technician role brought a sense of peace. I learned that when we finally align our actions with our purpose, everything else begins to fall into place. This chapter was a powerful reminder that true peace comes not from avoiding tough decisions but from making them with conviction and trust in ourselves.

Chapter 10: The Unexpected Call: Becoming a Financial Analyst

Life has a way of presenting unexpected opportunities, and this chapter taught me to stay open to them. Becoming a financial analyst wasn't something I had initially planned, but it ended up being a pivotal moment in my career. This reflection reminds me that sometimes, the most unexpected paths lead to the greatest growth. Keeping an open mind can bring new, fulfilling opportunities that align with both our professional and personal goals.

Chapter 11: Navigating Employee Rights and Assistance Programs (EAP & RA)

In navigating employee rights and assistance programs, I learned the power of self-advocacy. This chapter reinforced the importance of knowing your rights and using the resources available to protect your career. I realized that it's not just about standing up for yourself but also about educating yourself on the tools and support systems that are there to help you succeed. This knowledge became a powerful shield in my professional journey.

Chapter 12: Document, Document: The Power of Recordkeeping

The power of documentation cannot be overstated. In this chapter, I learned that keeping thorough records is not only a professional habit but a personal responsibility. Through detailed documentation, I was able to defend my rights and advocate for myself with confidence. This reflection reminds me that being organized and diligent in our work can make all the difference when challenges arise.

Chapter 13: Challenging Interactions and Behavioral Styles

Dealing with challenging interactions taught me invaluable lessons about patience, empathy, and assertiveness. This chapter highlighted the importance of understanding different behavioral styles and adapting my communication approach accordingly. I grew in my ability to manage conflict by staying calm and focused, recognizing that every interaction is an opportunity for growth, even when it feels difficult.

Chapter 14: Coping with Difficult Situations: Tools and Strategies

This chapter was about resilience and strategic thinking. I learned that coping with difficult situations requires not just emotional strength but also practical tools and approaches. By assessing the situation, understanding my reactions, and planning my next steps, I found that I could handle even the toughest challenges with grace. This reflection reminds me that we always have the power to choose how we respond, and that choice can make all the difference.

Chapter 15: Growth Through Adversity and New Beginnings

Looking back on my journey, I realized that every challenge I faced helped me grow into a stronger, more determined version of myself. Adversity, while painful, became the catalyst for personal and professional growth. This final chapter taught me that every ending is a new beginning, and with resilience, faith, and perseverance, we can rise above even the most difficult circumstances. Growth through adversity isn't just a lesson—it's a way of life.

Glossary

Term	Definition
Assertive Behavior	A communication style where individuals express their thoughts, feelings, and needs openly and honestly while respecting the rights of others.
Aggressive Behavior	A style of communication that involves expressing thoughts or feelings in a hostile, confrontational way that violates the rights of others.
Passive Behavior	A behavioral style characterized by reluctance or inability to express one's own thoughts, feelings, or needs, often prioritizing the desires of others.
Passive-Aggressive Behavior	A form of communication where individuals appear cooperative but harbor hidden resentment or anger often expressed indirectly through sarcasm or procrastination.
Employee Assistance Program (EAP)	A confidential program that offers employees and their families support with personal or work-related issues through

	counseling, resources, and consultations.
Reasonable Accommodation (RA)	Modifications or adjustments in the workplace that allow individuals with disabilities to perform their job duties effectively, ensuring equal employment opportunities.
Alternative Dispute Resolution (ADR)	A structured process is used to resolve workplace conflicts without formal litigation, often through methods like mediation or arbitration.
Hardship Transfer	A company policy allows employees to transfer to a different location or position due to personal or family hardships, such as medical emergencies or other significant life events.
Documentation	The process of recording workplace interactions, incidents, or conversations for future reference is especially useful in legal or conflict resolution contexts.
Mediation	A conflict resolution process in which a neutral third party facilitates communication between two parties in a dispute, with the goal of

	reaching a mutually acceptable solution.
Probation Officer	A law enforcement professional who is responsible for supervising individuals who are on probation, ensuring compliance with legal conditions set by the court.
Financial Technician	A professional who manages financial tasks such as budgeting, accounts payable/receivable, and financial reporting, typically within a government or corporate setting.
Union	An organization of workers is formed to protect and advance the rights and interests of its members, particularly in negotiations with employers.
Workplace Rights	The legal entitlements employees have in the workplace include the right to a safe work environment, fair compensation, and freedom from discrimination or harassment.
Resilience	The ability to recover from difficulties or challenges, using adversity as an opportunity for

	growth and personal development.
Self-Advocacy	The act of speaking up for oneself and standing up for one's rights, particularly in challenging or unfair situations.
Workplace Dynamics	The interactions, relationships, and power structures that exist within a workplace influence how employees collaborate, communicate, and manage conflict.
Sanctions	Penalties or disciplinary actions that are imposed by legal or organizational authorities when policies or agreements are violated.
Union Representation	The support and advocacy provided by a union on behalf of an employee, especially in legal disputes or during workplace negotiations.

Templates

Workplace Documentation Template

Use this template to document incidents, workplace issues, or any interactions that may need to be referenced in the future. It's important to keep detailed records for accuracy and professionalism.

Date	[Insert Date]
Time	[Insert Time]
Location	[Insert Location]
Individuals Involved	[List the individuals involved, including yourself and others]
Description of the Incident	[Describe the incident in detail. Include key facts such as what happened, who was involved, any relevant dialogue, and the sequence of events.]
Witnesses (if any)	[List any witnesses who were present]
Immediate Response/Actions Taken	[Detail how you or others responded immediately after the incident occurred.]
Follow-Up Actions	[Include any actions you took after the incident, such as reporting to a supervisor, filing a complaint, etc.]

Next Steps	[Identify what steps you plan to take next, if any. Consider follow-up meetings, further documentation, or formal reporting.]
Supporting Documents	[List or attach any supporting documents, emails, or other evidence.]
Signature	[Your Signature]

Communication Strategy Worksheet

Use this worksheet to prepare for a difficult conversation. Planning your approach helps you stay calm and focused, ensuring the conversation is productive.

Topic of Discussion	[What is the issue or topic that you need to address?]
Objective	[What is your main goal in having this conversation?]
Key Points to Address	[List 2-3 key points you need to communicate clearly during the conversation.]
Desired Outcome	[What do you hope the resolution or outcome will be?]
"I" Statements	[How will you frame your points using "I" statements to avoid sounding accusatory? Example: "I feel..." instead of "You never..."]
Anticipated Reactions	[How might the other person react? Identify possible responses and how you'll handle them.]
Listening Plan	[How will you ensure you actively listen to the other person's perspective? What questions might you ask to show engagement?]
Tone and Body Language	[How will you manage your tone and body language to keep the conversation calm and open?]

Next Steps	[What actions or follow-up will be required after the conversation?]

Goal-Setting Template

This template is designed to help you set and track personal or professional goals. Use it to outline your objectives, the steps needed to achieve them, and a timeline for completion.

Goal	[What is the specific goal you want to achieve?]
Why This Goal Matters	[Why is this goal important to you? What motivates you to achieve it?]
Steps to Achieve This Goal	[List the specific actions or steps required to accomplish this goal.]
Resources Needed	[What resources (time, skills, tools, support) will you need to achieve this goal?]
Potential Obstacles	[What challenges or obstacles do you anticipate? How will you overcome them?]
Support/Accountability	[Who can support you or hold you accountable for staying on track?]
Target Deadline	[Set a specific date for completing this goal.]
Milestones	[Identify smaller milestones along the way. Example:

	"Complete training by [date]" or "Submit proposal by [date]."
Progress Tracking	[How will you track your progress? Update this section regularly.]

www.ingramcontent.com/pod-product-compliance
Lightning Source LLC
LaVergne TN
LVHW061047070526
838201LV00074B/5208